A Guide to FREEDOM

A Guide to FREEDOM
11 Steps to Greater Joy, Hope, and Peace

ALICE BRIGGS

A Guide to Freedom
11 Steps to Greater Joy, Hope, and Peace

Copyright © 2016 by Alice Briggs

ISBN-13: 978-0692721650

All rights reserved. This book is protected by the copyright laws of the United States of America. This book may not be copied or reprinted for commercial gain or profit. The use of short quotations or occasional page copying for personal study is permitted. For any other use, written permission must be obtained from the author. Scripture quotations taken from the New American Standard Bible® (NASB), Copyright © 1960, 1962, 1963, 1968, 1971, 1972, 1973, 1975, 1977, 1995 by The Lockman Foundation Used by permission. www.Lockman.org

Alice Arlene, Ltd. Co. Press
PO Box 94825 Lubbock, TX 79493

CONTENTS

How to Use this Book vii
1   Grace for the Journey 1
2   Saturate Your Atmosphere 7
3   Read the Word 21
4   Personalizing Scripture 27
5   Listen to the Spirit 33
6   Take Negative Thoughts Captive 43
7   Bind up the Lies 49
8   Forgive Quickly and Often 55
9   A Community of Believers 63
10 Exercise Your Spiritual Giftings 71
11 Practice Thankfulness 79
12 A Brief Discussion of Splankna and SOZO 85
About the Author 89

Dedicated to all who are persevering and determined to walk in freedom. May this book give you more weapons in your arsenal to defeat the enemy so you can walk in glorious joy, abundant hope, and unwavering peace.

With great love and many thanks to my friends and family. A glorious blessing that truly has no words to describe. You all are such an incredible blessing to me.

HOW TO USE THIS BOOK

WELCOME TO THIS great adventure of freedom! I'm so pleased that you've purchased this book, or perhaps someone has done so for you. If you are anything like me, you're going to want to power through the whole thing. I'm going to ask you to refrain from doing exactly that. If you want to skim through, that's fine, get an overview of what this book has to offer. There may be a particular issue that is troubling you the most, or maybe you've been hearing people talk about one of the chapters and feel that this is where you need to start. I began to write this book in the order of the freedom guide that I give to my clients after they've had a session with me. When I wrote that guide, I had no idea that I would do anything more with it than that, so those points were in the order that they occurred to me at the time. I've rearranged them a bit for this book so hopefully they will have a more logical flow. You can work your way through from #1 to #11, or you can jump around.

If your inner healing practitioner or your counselor has given you this book, they might recommend you start working on this book at a certain point. While this book is not meant to replace sessions with your counselor or inner healing practitioner, it should enhance your work with your practitioner and reinforce the progress you make in between sessions. It will also be an excellent aid for those who have moved on to the next step after therapy. I have found within my practice as a therapist that clients who have previously done some of this work have less resistance to additional work and progress further, faster. But, this doesn't replace the need for such sessions.

If you are under the care of a counselor, minister, or practitioner, please follow their advice as how to use this book. The following recommendations are just that: recommendations based on what I have observed to be of most help to my clients. Your counselor, minister, or practitioner is far better able to tailor this workbook to fit your needs to ensure it benefits their treatment plan for you.

For those of you who are diving in on your own, welcome!!! You might find that this workbook is one that you could work through quite quickly. The chapters are not long, and the information is not complicated or difficult to understand. However, you will see the most benefits if you don't hurry through the book. Take some time and be willing to put into practice some of the suggestions I will be proposing. You can start at the beginning and work your way through, or you can begin with the chapter or chapters that fit where you are at in your life. But, start somewhere, and try my suggestions. It takes at least 28 days to make a new habit. So don't try something once or twice and decide that it isn't going to work. These aren't quick, instant fixes, but they are useful tools and skills you can learn.

Regardless of your plan of attack, please read "Grace for the Journey" first. If you can celebrate your victories while focusing on your next opportunity to succeed, you will experience much greater success in all the other tasks in the book.

A Guide to
FREEDOM

1

GRACE FOR THE JOURNEY

BEGINNING TO GIVE yourself grace is the first and best step you can take as you embark on this journey to freedom. The healing journey, regardless of length or depth, is a process, and I cannot encourage you enough to give yourself grace and mercy to not get it all right. Don't try to do everything at once, but do begin somewhere and keep moving forward. If you trip and fall, repent, and move on. One mistake is not a disaster. Indeed, an entire series of mistakes need not be a disaster if you get up again and keep moving forward.

Self-criticism toward the mistakes and progress I have made on my journey has been difficult at times, but once I adopted the strategy of grace, the rewards have been remarkable. Celebrating every little bit of progress, regardless of how small it seems, has proven to be one of the best ways I have found to overcome self-criticism. I had a lifelong habit of being very hard on myself. Perfectionism is a brutal taskmaster. It always focuses on what you haven't done and how far you still have to go.

I might have heard about the "Celebrating Your Progress' technique before, but it really sank in as I watched an inspirational teaching by Abi Stumvoll, a pastor at Bethel Church, Redding California via Livestream. Abi leans toward perfectionism and has found one key to freedom from perfectionism is to celebrate every victory and all successes—no matter how small. Whenever she did a certain thing as opposed to not doing that certain thing, she was winning. To follow her train of thought—if I go for a walk I wanted to take, as opposed to not going for the walk, I'm winning! If I only go for a walk twice this week, I'm still winning, even if I had planned on going for a walk three times this week. Two walks are more than I would have done if I hadn't gone at all!

Abi found that success is motivating. I'm also finding that to be true. I mean, seriously, does castigating yourself ever make you want to do better the next time? Personally, castigating myself just makes me want to crawl into a hole and hide. It only reinforces the 'why should I bother; I'm losing anyhow' attitude.

So, what does "Celebrating Victories" look like for me?

I can get upset with myself because I bought another lie of the enemy. I can get overwhelmed and discouraged that there is so much to get free from, and it's going too slowly. Or, I can rejoice that I spoke the truth over myself. I'm winning! I read five verses in my Bible yesterday. I'm winning! I went ten minutes without a negative thought. I'm winning!

You will notice that I did not say that I always listen to the truth or that I always read five chapters a day in my Bible. What I haven't done, isn't the point. The point is I have done something towards my goals. I'm winning! I focus on what I have accomplished. I don't focus on what I have not yet done.

As I rejoice over the small accomplishments, do you know what happens? They lead to bigger ones. I begin to look for the small steps that I can do, and do those small steps, rather than become discouraged by what I haven't yet done.

For example, if I choose one of the suggestions presented in this guide to freedom, and I focus on doing that 'one thing' even if I only do that 'one thing' one time, I'm winning! Maybe I'll do it twice tomorrow; I'm winning! If I do it three times next week, but twice the week after, I'm still winning!

I'm doing better than before I started when I didn't ever do it. Do you see how fun this is?!

Action Points:

1. Celebrate any victory that you achieve, regardless of size or impact.
2. Take note of where you are now, and celebrate any further progress towards more freedom.
3. Set goals, yes, but set small ones at first! Set goals with smaller bite-sized steps you can achieve.
4. As you achieve one area of victory, add another, and so on until you are truly free!

Are you a chart person? Or perhaps you are a list person. Here are a couple sample charts and lists that might help you as you begin to keep track of your progress.

I'm Winning!

Goal: Measurable & Concrete

S	W	T	W	T	F	S

Set rewards for successful completion of one week, two weeks, one month, or whatever is appropriate for your goal.

I will celebrate _____ completed by _____
I will celebrate _____ completed by _____
I will celebrate _____ completed by _____

Celebrate your successes!

I'm Winning!

Goal: Measurable & Concrete

```
Jan   1 2 3 4 5 6 7 8 9 10 11 12 13 14 15 16 17 18 19 20 21 22 23 24 25 26 27 28 29 30 31
Feb   1 2 3 4 5 6 7 8 9 10 11 12 13 14 15 16 17 18 19 20 21 22 23 24 25 26 27 28 29
Mar   1 2 3 4 5 6 7 8 9 10 11 12 13 14 15 16 17 18 19 20 21 22 23 24 25 26 27 28 29 30 31
Apr   1 2 3 4 5 6 7 8 9 10 11 12 13 14 15 16 17 18 19 20 21 22 23 24 25 26 27 28 29 30
May   1 2 3 4 5 6 7 8 9 10 11 12 13 14 15 16 17 18 19 20 21 22 23 24 25 26 27 28 29 30 31
Jun   1 2 3 4 5 6 7 8 9 10 11 12 13 14 15 16 17 18 19 20 21 22 23 24 25 26 27 28 29 30
Jul   1 2 3 4 5 6 7 8 9 10 11 12 13 14 15 16 17 18 19 20 21 22 23 24 25 26 27 28 29 30 31
Aug   1 2 3 4 5 6 7 8 9 10 11 12 13 14 15 16 17 18 19 20 21 22 23 24 25 26 27 28 29 30 31
Sept  1 2 3 4 5 6 7 8 9 10 11 12 13 14 15 16 17 18 19 20 21 22 23 24 25 26 27 28 29 30
Oct   1 2 3 4 5 6 7 8 9 10 11 12 13 14 15 16 17 18 19 20 21 22 23 24 25 26 27 28 29 30 31
Nov   1 2 3 4 5 6 7 8 9 10 11 12 13 14 15 16 17 18 19 20 21 22 23 24 25 26 27 28 29 30
Dec   1 2 3 4 5 6 7 8 9 10 11 12 13 14 15 16 17 18 19 20 21 22 23 24 25 26 27 28 29 30 31
```

Highlight the days you win

Set rewards for successful completion of one week, two weeks, one month, or whatever is appropriate for your goal.

I will celebrate _____ completed by _____

I will celebrate _____ completed by _____

I will celebrate _____ completed by _____

Celebrate your successes!

I'M WINNING!

Goal: Measurable & Concrete

Give yourself a star for each time you succeed.

Set rewards for successful completion of 10, 20, 50, or whatever is appropriate for your goal.

I will celebrate _____ completed by _____
I will celebrate _____ completed by _____
I will celebrate _____ completed by _____

Celebrate your successes!

2

SATURATE YOUR ATMOSPHERE

WHY WORSHIP? THE Lord inhabits the praise of His people (Psalm 22:3). Paul and Silas praised while they were imprisoned and in bonds. As they prayed and sang, their bonds were loosened as well as the bonds of their fellow prisoners who overheard their worship (Acts 16:23-26). In 2 Chronicles 20:18-24, God delivered His people from their enemies as they worshipped the Lord.

When we worship, we turn our focus from our difficulties and toward God and His greatness. I've heard it said that as we worship, we see our challenges in perspective, as we concentrate on the bigness of God, we rightly see our problems as small as they really are. There are times I know this to be true. However, sometimes I think that this type of statement is often used to minimize the effects of truly traumatic events and occurrences. Yes, God is bigger than anything that happens to us. However, this does not mitigate the significance of our hurts. God wants to walk with us through hard times. During my darkest times, worship reminds me of His closeness and His comfort. I take courage in songs that were written by those who have walked through challenging times themselves.

There is something tangible that happens when we saturate our atmosphere with worship music. I'm not entirely sure of all of the whys and hows, but perhaps quantum physics has something to do with it. Worship resonates at a frequency that seems to transfer itself into the structure and atmosphere of the place where it is released. It lingers long past the time that the last note died away. I've visited churches and cathedrals where God has been worshipped for hundreds of years. There's something unique in the very atmosphere of many of them.

Based on my earlier experiences in those ancient houses of worship, when I was later introduced to the benefits of saturating the atmosphere of my home with worship music, it made sense. "What could hurt?" I thought. I was going through a difficult time, and I needed all the help I could get to keep moving forward. And so, I listened to Christian radio 24/7. As I did, I began to notice a difference in my home. There was lightness in my house that I didn't feel elsewhere.

When you are using music to shift atmospheres, I don't think the style of music matters as much as the heart and Spirit from which the musicians perform. I have found worship music to be most effective. Although I enjoy most Christian music, I realize that not all Christian music is worship. When I need to shift my atmosphere, I listen to music that I sense the Spirit in the most.

Some of my current favorite worship artists are: Bethel Music, The Torwalts, Kim Walker-Smith, and the Helsers. A friend curates a free Youtube channel with great music: http://www.youtube.com/playlist?list=PL7AC045DAFB932407

My friend, Del Hungerford, is a musician who records music with the pitch tuned to A432. This pitch is found in the sounds of nature and the cosmos. Del believes that music played within this frequency is healing. To help set the atmosphere in my office during sessions, I have begun to play her music. As it is instrumental, it works well. Her songs are 25-30 minutes each, and they flow well from one to the other. You can find more information on her website: healingfrequenciesmusic.com. If you use the coupon code A=432 or sign up for her newsletter, you will receive a free download of one of her songs.

Along with another friend, Del and I are currently researching frequencies of music and how they relate to color and healing. Some of our research has revealed substantial evidence as to why playing music shifts your atmosphere. As a person of faith, I accept that there are many things that I will not fully grasp. However, as I have a scientific background, I do so love when I discover something that suggests a reason why something is so.

For example, If you take two tuning forks and hit them so that they vibrate, the one vibrating at the lower frequency will gradually begin to come into alignment with the one that is vibrating at the higher frequency.

There has been some research that states that more positive emotions correlate to higher frequencies. Love resonates higher than fear, etc. By saturating your atmosphere with music that utilizes these higher frequencies, you could be releasing an atmosphere that welcomes more positive emotions. While more research needs to be done to confirm these findings, it does hold some interesting possibilities.

Action points:
1. Find a Christian radio station near you.
2. Try listening to the YouTube soaking list I mentioned.
3. Try listening to some of my other suggestions of artists.
4. Begin to play your choice of artist/music at strategic times, or all of the time if you so desire.
5. Take note of the shift in the atmosphere around you as you listen to various artists.

Experiment:
1. Pick a place that you are in frequently and where you have the ability to play music in, even if it is played softly: home, office, car, etc.
2. Make note of what music, if any, is played there now.
3. How do you feel when you are there?
4. What is the behavior of the others around you?
5. What do you sense while there?

6. Next time you are away from there, note how you are feeling and what you are sensing before you enter the place. Then, make note of anything that changes when you enter.

This is your baseline data, be as descriptive as possible, although that might be difficult at first.

Now, choose some uplifting Christian music to play as often as possible in that space. If you already play music in that space, choose another artist, style, or genre for your experiment. Play the music for a week and then, once again, go through the questions listed above. Make note of any differences. Continue this experiment for another two weeks and then for one month. What do you discover? Was there a significant difference? I'd love to hear your results. If you chose Del Hungerford's music, do let me know what your experience was, and I'll pass on your experiences to her.

I've included data collection sheets if you wish to quantify your findings in any way.

Saturate Your Atmosphere Data Collection

Baseline Data:

Prior to beginning, take note of the following, and anything else that occurs to you. The change may be slow and subtle at times, so this information will be a helpful comparison to the final data.

What is your target location? Where will this experiment take place?

_____
_____

What music is playing now, if any?

_____
_____
_____

What are you feeling? On a scale of 1 to 10, 10 being the most prevalent emotion, how would you rank those feelings?

_____
_____
_____

Take note of the behavior of the people and animals who inhabit or frequent this space. Also make note of the frequency of any specific behaviors. For example: The dog barks incessantly 3x/day, or my child yells in anger 4x/week, or my coworker complains of a headache 3x/day, etc.

_____
_____
_____

Is there anything in particular that you sense when you are in this space? How does that differ from when you are somewhere else?

_____
_____
_____
_____
_____

The experiment begins on this day: _____

What music will you play? How often will it be played? The longer you can play the music, the better. However, it doesn't need to be so loud that it intrudes on other activities going on in the space.

_____
_____
_____

Hopefully, a couple of weeks, or even after only a few days, you will notice a significant, positive difference in this space. Expand your experiment with other music and in other spaces. I've given you data collection charts at 2 and 4 weeks, and two other charts for extended periods. You might want to extend your experiment to cover a period of 2 months, 4 months, etc.

2 Week Data Point:

Date _____

Think back to the feelings you noted at the beginning, what number on the scale of 1 to 10 would you give them now?

_____
_____
_____
_____
_____

Are there any other feelings that you are noticing that weren't present at the beginning of the experiment? Rank them on the same scale.

_____
_____
_____
_____
_____

Think back to the behaviors you noted that were taking place in the setting you are performing this experiment. Think about how often those behaviors occurred at the beginning. What is the frequency of those behaviors now?

_____
_____
_____
_____
_____

Are there other behaviors that you are seeing now that you want to make note of?

_____
_____
_____
_____
_____

What do you sense now, in this space? Does it feel the same? Is it different? How so?

_____
_____
_____
_____
_____

4-Week Data Point:

Date _____

Remembering the feelings you noted at the beginning of your experiment, what number on the scale of 1 to 10 would you give those feelings now?

_____
_____
_____
_____
_____

Are there any other feelings that you are noticing now that are new? Rank them on the same scale.

_____
_____
_____
_____
_____

Think back to the behaviors you noted that were taking place in the setting you are performing this experiment. Think about how often those behaviors occurred at the beginning. What is the frequency of those behaviors now?

_____
_____
_____
_____
_____

Are there other behaviors that you are seeing now that you want to make note of?

_____
_____
_____
_____
_____

What do you sense now, in this space? Is it the same? Is it different?

_____
_____
_____
_____
_____

Extended Period of Time

Date _____

Of the feelings you noted at the beginning, what number on the scale of 1 to 10 would you give them now?

_____
_____
_____
_____
_____

Are there any other feelings that you are noticing that are new? Rank them on the same scale.

_____
_____
_____
_____
_____

Of the behaviors and frequencies that you noted at the beginning, make note of the frequency of those behaviors now.

_____
_____
_____
_____
_____

Are there other behaviors that you are seeing now that you want to make note of?

_____
_____
_____
_____
_____

What do you sense now, in this space? Is it the same? Is it different?

_____
_____
_____
_____
_____

Saturating the Atmosphere Chart

	Before	2 Weeks	4 Weeks			
Date						
Music						
Feeling & Scale 1-10						
Behavior/ Frequency						
Anything else you sense in the space						

3

READ THE WORD

THE BIBLE HAS much to say about itself. If we hide the Word in our hearts, it will help us not to sin (Ps 119:11). It is the sword of the Spirit, the only offensive weapon against the enemy given us for our spiritual armor in Ephesians 6:17. It is a lamp to our feet and light for our path (Ps 119:105).

The Bible is also the best place that I know to learn about how God has worked with and through people since the beginning of time. We can learn much about who God is and what He is like by reading his Word. By reading from several different translations and paraphrases, you see the Word with fresh eyes!

I'm not saying that you need to study the Bible for hours a day to receive any benefit. That's just not a realistic goal for most of us. However, there are many ways you can feast on God's Word. Here are a few examples: You can subscribe to KLOVE radio's verse of the day. I've been receiving KLOVE's emails for 15 years or so now. I also just subscribed to a daily Proverb through bibleplan.org. They have quite several plans to choose from. I enjoy the convenience of having these Bible readings land in my inbox each morning, especially when traveling. Encouraging Bible Quotes is another great online resource as the website includes Topical Verse Indexes and several do-it-yourself Bible Reading plans.

If you have a longer daily commute to work, or you have time to listen to the Bible but not time to read it, Daily Audio Bible is a great resource to be aware of. Brian Hardin has been reading the Bible as a podcast every day since 2006. He reads from a different version every week, and if you listen every day, you will have heard the entire Bible within a year. Daily Audio Bible has a flourishing community of listeners who pray for one another's needs and support each other via social media.

A quick search on the Internet will lead you to Bible Reading Plans for most translations. You can read the Bible through in a year, or you can take your time and read it over a period of three years, for example. The New Living Translation published a Bible that is arranged to guide you through a daily reading plan to cover the entire Bible in a year. Some Bibles are arranged chronologically, some are arranged in the traditional order, beginning (Genesis 1) and going straight through to Revelations. Other Bibles are arranged so you read a cross section of scriptures each day. If you are new to reading the Bible, I would suggest getting started by reading the gospels of John and/or Mark. Both these gospels chronicle Jesus' time on earth, and both will provide you with a good overview of His life and purpose.

If you're artistic and like to doodle, there's a movement growing that involves creating art in a Bible itself, as it relates to the portion you are reading. Rebekah Jones, a creative Christian artist, has developed a challenge related to artistic Bible journaling. She also offers online tutorials and other resources, if this technique of Bible study interests you, you might want to drop by her website. Despite my artistic bent, this method of Bible Journaling is not something that I've personally explored, but from what I hear, many find that God meets them while applying this methodology of Creative Bible Study. He is, after all, the Creator, and He seems to enjoy it when we create things as well.

I've also expanded my study of the Word through topical and word studies. I visit online concordances such as Bible Gateway or Blue Letter Bible and look up all the verses that pertain to a given topic or word. You can do the same with the names of God. Perhaps you are struggling with a particular emotion. It might be helpful to do a word study on that emotion to see what the Bible has to say about it.

There is also the option just to pick up a Bible and start to read, and read as God speaks to your situation!

When something seems to leap right off the page of your Bible, make note of it. Underline, highlight, or doodle in your Bible in whatever method works best for you. By doing so, it will help you remember that this is a time when God spoke directly to you and your situation. I like to put dates in the margins of my Bible and a brief note as to what was going on in my life at the time I highlighted the verse. If privacy is an issue, create a unique shorthand or code. I love going through my old Bibles and remembering how God spoke to me through His word, right when I needed to hear it! Personalizing Bible verses is another technique you might want to consider. I'll talk about that more in the next chapter.

Action Points:
1. Find a hardcopy version of the Bible, or download a Bible app.
2. Sign up for one of the suggestions above.
3. Set a goal to read more than you are doing now.
4. Do a topical study on a topic that interests you.
5. Do a topic and/or word study regarding a struggle you are having.

Read the Word Goal Sheet

If you want to increase the amount you are reading of the Bible:

Today's Date: _____

How much do you read now?

_____

What is a doable amount that you can add to what you are doing now? More verses? Read more frequently?

_____
_____
_____

What is your plan for accomplishing this? An app? Email list? Purchasing a study Bible or Journaling Bible? Setting reminders on your phone?

_____
_____
_____

Choose one of the calendars or charts in Chapter 1 to make note of the times you are successful.

Set reward points along the way. For example: After I've read at least ____ verses each day for ____ days (not necessarily consecutively, but it could be), I will reward myself with:

_____
_____
_____

A Sample Topical Bible Study Format

Pick a topic, word, concept, lie, etc. that you want to research:

_____

Utilize a search function on a Bible study website, or a concordance to look up references pertaining to that topic. You will likely need many more lines than I've provided below. Feel free to photocopy this page, or if you prefer, make a similar chart in your journal.

Reference   What does this passage say about this topic?

_____

What is God saying to me:

4

PERSONALIZING SCRIPTURE

AT TIMES, A verse jumps out at me as I read the Bible. That verse seems to directly apply to what I'm currently going through, it answers a question that I have, or it speaks about something that I desire to see manifest in my life. Not only do I highlight those verses, but I also personalize them. By doing so, I seem to absorb the truths of those verses more readily.

I have found it helpful to keep a stack of 3x5 index cards at hand as I read the Bible. I then write those verse or verses that leap off the page on the cards. I personalize the verses as if they were written directly to me by inserting my name as much into the text as it would fit. I then read those verses aloud to myself as often as needed. During particularly dark times in my life, I discovered so many verses I could personalize that that I placed the cards in a photo album so I could more easily flip through the treasures I found.

For example: Psalm 100:4–"Enter his gates with thanksgiving; go into his courts with praise; give thanks to him and praise his name."

There are at least two ways to personalize this verse. I could say: "I will enter his gates with thanksgiving. I will go into his courts with praise. I will give thanks to him and I will praise his name."

Or I could say: "Alice will enter his gates with thanksgiving. Alice will go into his courts with praise. Alice will give thanks to him and Alice will praise his name."

I find the latter application is most effective.

By personalizing verses, I find a deeper personal connection to what the Scripture is saying to me. As I grew up in church, I have been reading the Bible as long as I can remember. It's easy for me to miss things that God might have for for me in a certain passage simply because I am so familiar with a passage. However, when I take the time to personalize the verse(s), I am encouraged (or challenged!) in a new and different way by what I'm reading. Personalizing the Scriptures helps me to "own" those special verses. They aren't just something someone a couple thousand years ago wrote. These words are what God is saying to me right here and now.

Romans 10:17 says that hearing the Word produces more faith, therefore I often read the Bible out loud. I don't know exactly how this produces more faith, it may have something to do with increasing the sensory input, or perhaps it has something to do with quantum physics. Whatever the reason, I have found reading the Word out loud to be of great benefit. There is something powerful about hearing the Word.

Theoretically, writing longhand, that is, putting pen to paper, makes a greater connection with your mental processes than typing on a keyboard. There are those who recommend keeping a handwritten journal for this reason. I also find it easier to hand write verses on a 3x5 card than try and print on it.

I chose 3x5 index cards probably as a throwback to writing projects I did in school before Google and the World Wide Web ever existed. They are a nice size to write most verses out and they are sturdy enough to flip through often without worrying they will fall apart. You can prop them up next to your coffee/tea pot, tape them to the bathroom mirror, or wherever you find a spot that allows you to see them frequently. By keeping a stack of these cards in the car to flip through while stuck in traffic you make good use of time and you might even help your blood pressure level!

Personalizing Scripture

Meditating on Scripture is another way to make the truth contained in the Bible become alive and active in your life. As you think about each verse and insert your name into that verse, what is your response? I don't mean the response that you think you should have, I mean your honest, gut-level response. It may not be a positive one, and that's okay. God knows the deepest things about us, things that we don't necessarily always know about ourselves. He is not going to be shocked or stunned by any of our responses. He longs to meet us in that point of honesty, reveal the truth to us, and heal the wounds that cause us to doubt His Word. If you feel a particular verse doesn't resonate or ring true to you as you meditate upon it, ask God why that is. He may bring to mind a memory or thought process that is preventing His truth from getting through. We often read God's through the lens of our woundedness and we need His help to hear what He is really saying to us. Don't be afraid to ask Him what the truth is about the Bible verse. God uses a variety of ways to show those areas in our hearts that hinder us from accepting the wonderful truths found in His Word. You may need additional help in getting to all of the layers, if so, I recommend that you seek out someone who is trained in Biblically-based inner healing. I will discuss the subject of inner healing in a later chapter, but for now, be reassured that God desires your freedom even more than you do and He provides a myriad of ways to bring that freedom to you.

Action Points:
1. Get some 3x5 cards.
2. Find some verses that speak to you and your current situation.
3. Set a reminder on your phone to review these verses.
4. Post the cards where you will see them often.
5. Add verses to your stash as often as you can.

Ready to try? I'll give you a couple of my favorite verses. You can fill in the blanks to personalize the verses.

> The enemy comes to steal, kill and destroy from _____. But, Jesus has come to give _____ life, and life abundantly. John 10:10

For I know the plans I have for _____. Plans to prosper _____ and not to harm _____. Plans to give _____ a hope and a future. Jeremiah 29:11

This is My Verse

Reference:

This is My Verse

Reference:

This is My Verse

Reference:

This is My Verse

Reference:

5

LISTEN TO THE SPIRIT

TAKING THE TIME to listen to the Spirit is an excellent way to gain more freedom. Two-way journaling is a great way to refine your listening. I learned this technique by watching Dr. Mark Virkler's 4 Keys to Hearing God's Voice DVDs.

Make sure your heart is right, and then ask God a question, such as: "What do you think of me?" or "How do you see me?" Just quiet yourself, then listen. Write down whatever you hear. Don't analyze, just write. Try to resist the urge to proofread your writing until after this exercise is completed. Spiritual activities such as this one tend to register on the right side of your brain. Analyzation and proofreading are more left brain activities. For those of us who spend a lot of time using the left side of our brain, switching to the right takes practice, so stay over there as long as you can when you get there!

If this method of journaling and hearing from God is something new to you, it is Dr. Virkler's recommendation that you run your journaling by a few advisors who know and love you. They should be people who you feel are proficient in hearing from God for themselves. I think Dr. Virkler's advice is sound and I encourage you to follow it, especially if you are making a major decision of any kind. When you first step out in journaling and listening to God's voice, it's reassuring and wise to check with those you trust, by asking them if they think that what you've heard is indeed the voice of the Spirit.

There are many different ways to hear the Spirit, and God seems to use a different vocabulary for each of us. He speaks 'our' language. I've always enjoyed numbers, so that's one way He speaks to me. Clock times are often code words for Bible verses between God and I. He also speaks to me through cloud formations. Cloud gazing reminds me of childhood and the joy I felt as I picked out shapes in the sky. The shape of a dove in the clouds reminds me to be at peace and not worry. I often see that image!

Traveling or seeing in the Spirit is something that I enjoy doing and that I find very helpful. It is similar to two-way journaling, but this is more visual and involves a sanctified use of the imagination, hence the name! I close my eyes and visit the secret place God has created for just for Him and me. This place is unique to each individual, but it is a place to go and meet with any or all members of the Trinity. My secret place is typically a hidden meadow with a lake that I access by walking on a pathway through a forest. This spot is reminiscent of childhood memories of Houghton Lake in Michigan and the mountains around Ruidoso, New Mexico. Sometimes, Jesus meets me on the shore of the lake where he seems to enjoy skipping stones. These generally appear to be gemstones, and he laughs at my surprise that he would throw large rubies, sapphires, and diamonds into the water.

Sometimes, he teaches me to pray from a place of peace and rest and so we swing in hammocks and watch the clouds roll by. Other times, the whole Trinity shows up, and we sit around a bonfire making S'mores. The painting above looks similar to my secret place. I painted it during a worship session at a local House of Prayer. It was a bit startling to find such a personal space appearing before me as I painted. (To learn more about the process of this painting, I invite you to visit my art blog at alicearlene.com.)

When seeing in the Spirit, I write what I am experiencing in a journal document on my computer to the best of my ability. As I can type without looking at the keyboard, this works well for me. I find it helpful to record what I see as I see it, as it is easy to forget details after the fact. If you aren't able to type while you are in the secret place, pull out your cell phone and make a voice memo. You can transcribe it later. If all else fails, make it a point to write down as much as you can as soon as you get back.

If I have a question in mind, I bring that issue with me to the secret place and wait for His answer. I find that this is an invaluable tool, not just for finding freedom, but also for pursuing my destiny.

Hopefully, the following will give you an idea of what I mean when writing a detailed journal about my experiences. This is just a snippet from a journal entry I made as I went to the secret place. I won't put all of it here because it wouldn't be appropriate. In answer to the question that might be on your mind, yes, I did go back and edit for clarity after I finished:

> I see the sun sparkling on the ripples on the water that is caused by the wind. It is a sweet breeze. If I look up, I can see the distant shore of the lake. It doesn't appear to be a lake that I've been to before. There are evergreen trees around most of the lake, with a few patches of aspen here and there. The shore is very grassy, and the lake appears to get deep fairly quickly. There are other people there, but they are very far away. I can hear the wind rustling through the pine trees. There is such a sweetness to the wind, that I am sure there is some mint growing somewhere nearby. I think we are somewhere in the mountains, as I can see their peaks rising up beyond the trees. I think that most of them are behind us. I see clouds floating over the valley of the lake. Peaceful, white, fluffy clouds. I look at Jesus, and he is wearing jeans and a white shirt, and hiking shoes. I see a backpack behind us, and I think that it is His for a minute. He twinkles His eyes at me, and I realize that He has no need for a backpack. It is mine and it looks battered and worn. I now remember how heavy it was to carry. I feel the lightness of the lack of it on my shoulders.
>
> (We talk about the contents of the backpack, some of which related to people and situations for which I was interceding at the time.)

Jesus stands beside me. He takes my hand, then puts His arm around me and hugs me tightly. I am aware that my backpack is no longer there. I look at Jesus and He cocks an eyebrow at me for feeling a bit sad about that. I take a deep breath and laugh. Jesus laughs with me, and we can hear the echoes of our laughter joining in all around us. Jesus looks at me, kisses my forehead and sends me home.

"Leave your burdens here, dear one," He says as the vision fades.

The benefits of learning to hear the Spirit and visiting the places God shows you, is that they give you the opportunity to learn more about the character and love of God. Regardless of what images the word father conjures in your head, our Heavenly Father is a very good one. Visualization and experiences such as going to the secret place cements a truth far more than merely reading about that truth.

Action Points:

1. Read one of the books listed above.
2. Practice journaling with God.
3. Practice seeing in the Spirit.

Journaling prompts:

1. A secret place walk through: Choose a comfortable position. Many people report playing worship music in the background is very helpful for this exercise. (See Chapter 2: Saturate Your Atmosphere for recommendations.) You might want a pillow or a light blanket. Close your eyes. Picture yourself walking down a path. There is a fork in the road, and you can choose if you want to go towards the trees, or into the meadow. Can you hear the birds singing overhead? Can you smell the flowers blooming along the path? You can stop and pick some if you'd like. Continue to go along your chosen path. You hear the sound of a brook or a small river in the distance; it chuckles as it tumbles over the stones in its bed. You decide to investigate, and

luckily, the path seems to be taking you in that direction. You walk until you come around a bend, and there you see the water, sparkling in the sunlight. The water looks so cool and refreshing, and your feet are a bit warm from the walk, so you slip out of your shoes, and start to wade into the river.

Choose the member of the Trinity with whom you feel the most comfortable with, and invite them to come and meet you here. Stay in this place of rest and allow them to meet with you. Try not to ask too many questions. Simply ask what they would like to say to you or show you in this place.

When you get back, write down what you heard, saw, felt, or did. For some of us, this kind of thing comes easily. It wasn't easy for me at first; I was trying too hard. All I felt was a sense of peace and acceptance, and that was perfectly fine. This is just one way that God might reveal Himself to you; it is certainly not the only way. Nevertheless, don't give up right away. Sometimes, it takes a while for our internal dialogue to quiet down enough so that we can hear Him. The Scriptures speak of the benefits of waiting on the Lord.

2. Take one of the personalized Scriptures that you discovered in the previous chapters of this workbook, and quietly sit before the Lord while meditating on that Scripture. Ask Him if there's anything about that scripture that He would like to share with you. Still your heart and mind and listen to what He says.
3. Ask Him what lie you believe about yourself. Then, ask Him what the truth is.

Disclaimer: Depending on the type and severity of your woundings, you might find that this type of activity is triggering for you. If that is the case, I recommend that you get in touch with someone trained in SOZO or Splankna, or any other Bible-based inner healing ministry. (I'm trained in both SOZO and Splankna, so I'm familiar with these methods. While I am not as familiar with other Christian inner healing methodologies, I've heard good things about several.) There are times when we need the help of others to successfully heal. We all need help at times and this truth shouldn't be a cause for blame or shame. Often, an outside perspective is critical to our success when we encounter one of those "stuck" places we all seem to stumble upon at one point or another in our lives.

Listen to the Spirit Journal Page

Date: _____

This is my question, or the issue on my heart during this time:

_____
_____
_____
_____
_____

Father, Jesus, Holy Spirit: What do you have to say about this?

_____
_____
_____
_____
_____
_____
_____
_____
_____
_____
_____
_____
_____
_____
_____
_____
_____
_____

Listen to the Spirit Journal Page

Date: _____

This is my question, or the issue on my heart during this time:

_____
_____
_____
_____
_____

Father, Jesus, Holy Spirit: What do you have to say about this?

_____
_____
_____
_____
_____
_____
_____
_____
_____
_____
_____
_____
_____
_____
_____
_____

Listen to the Spirit Journal Page

Date: _____

This is my question, or the issue on my heart during this time:

_____
_____
_____
_____
_____

Father, Jesus, Holy Spirit: What do you have to say about this?

_____
_____
_____
_____
_____
_____
_____
_____
_____
_____
_____
_____
_____
_____
_____
_____
_____
_____
_____
_____

Listen to the Spirit Journal Page

Date: _____

This is my question, or the issue on my heart during this time:

_____
_____
_____
_____
_____

Father, Jesus, Holy Spirit: What do you have to say about this?

_____
_____
_____
_____
_____
_____
_____
_____
_____
_____
_____
_____
_____
_____
_____
_____

6

TAKE NEGATIVE THOUGHTS CAPTIVE

AS YOU STUDY Scripture and internalize the truth, you will begin to notice other thoughts that enter your mind. In this chapter, I hope to teach you how to get rid of those negative thoughts. As these thoughts come across your mind, immediately take them captive. Tell them no, and declare the opposite (the truth!) over yourself and your situation.

These negative thoughts will be unique to each of us, which can make them tricky to discover. If we all had the same fears and worries, then I could tell you to beware of a standardized list of lies or negative thoughts, and that would be the end of it. However, it's not as easy as that.

There are usually three sources of thoughts in our heads. They all can sound like us, so we need to learn to discern the source of each. If you have more than three, then you are possibly dealing with an alter/fragment/part, and that is beyond the scope of this chapter. The normative three voices are your own voice, the Lord's voice, and the enemy's voice. A big clue as to which voice belongs to the enemy is given in John 10:10 "The enemy comes to steal, kill, and destroy; but I came that you might have life abundantly." (Alice's paraphrase) So, we can line up any given thought against this verse to determine its source.

The Lord's voice will always be consistent with Scriptural principles. Notice that I didn't say that everything that He says to you as you pray and seek His Spirit will be found in the Bible. However, you've probably already discovered the Bible doesn't discuss electricity, cars, which person you should marry, what occupation you should choose, etc. My test is not trying to find the exact words that I felt God speak to me through seeking His spirit in the Bible. However, God's voice will be consistent with the principles and foundational truths He already mentioned throughout the Bible. This is why reading the Bible and personalizing Scriptures is so important.

The first clue that a thought or an emotion is coming from the enemy is that that thought or emotion is contrary to Biblical principles. The enemy utilizes feelings of doubt, fear, pressure, condemnation, and a general lack of peace, to name a few. He is the father of all lies, and although he some understanding of truth, he only uses a snippet of truth as bait so that you will buy into a greater lie. He is the master of twisting the truth for his gain.

Our voices will sound like us, and our voice often speaks from how we view life based on our experiences. As we become free, and as we become closer to Christ, our minds will be renewed, and our voice will start to sound very similar to the Father's.

So, just what does it mean to take a thought captive? It simply means that we will not allow a negative or damaging thought to linger in our minds. Once you recognize that a thought is coming from the enemy, just say "No! Nope! Nada!" Speak out loud if need be. Follow that refusal to allow that thought to stay with a statement where you bind up that thought and cast it on the cross. As that thought is neither mine nor a thought from God, I will not receive it. I then focus on the appropriate thought (truth) that counteracts that thought. I make use of my personalized scriptures, these verses gives me strength and power, helping me to focus on the truth and create positive thoughts.

If this is a recurrent thought pattern, see if you can pinpoint the environment you might be in when you are more likely to hear it. You can then proactively release the truth before you enter into that environment. I don't recommend trying to confront demonic influences over places or environments by yourself. That's a whole other topic for another day, but suffice it to say, it is not wise to do something along those lines unless you are confident that you have the authority to do so.

However, we, as believers DO have the authority to bless our environment, and to release the Presence of God wherever we go. He is in and with us at all times. Make a conscious effort to release those truths that align with the heart and mind of God when you are in those places. You don't need to make big show of it, and it doesn't need to be a big deal. It can be as simple as quietly speaking under your breath, "I release the spirit of peace (or whatever) in this place." "Lord, let your presence rest in this place." "Holy Spirit, come to this place."

Action Points:
1. Is there a negative thought that crosses your mind frequently?
2. Is there any part of your life that you have no hope of good for the future?
3. Make note of the thoughts that cross your mind, especially those that come out of nowhere.
4. Determine who is the source of those thoughts.
5. Replace any negative thoughts with positive, godly thoughts.

Taking Thoughts Captive

The thought that is troubling me:

_____

Search the Scriptures to discover what God has to say about this:

_____
_____
_____
_____
_____

What is God saying to ME about this subject?

_____
_____
_____
_____
_____
_____
_____
_____

I bind up this thought that:

_____
_____
_____
_____

Take Negative Thoughts Captive

I cast it to the cross along with any and all entities that are involved in this thought in any way. I will not partner with you, and I revoke any and all agreements that I've made with this thought. I gather all of that up, and I cast it on the cross of Jesus. I place the blood of Jesus between all of that and me, and I accept and choose to believe the truth that:

_____
_____
_____
_____
_____
_____
_____
_____
_____
_____

Read through this prayer as often as this negative thought troubles you. If this is a thought that you frequently struggle with, personalize a few of the Scriptures you found above that speak to you the most. Don't be afraid to read those bible verses as often needed until the truth sinks in.

7

BIND UP THE LIES

AS WE BECOME more comfortable in the techniques used to take negative thoughts captive, the next step is to bind up the lies of the enemy. That's easier said than done sometimes! However, as you progress in this book, you should begin to notice it is easier for you to discern what is coming from you, what is God, and what is the enemy.

Anything that worries you or causes you to experience fear and anxiety is under the influence of a lie from the enemy. Remember, his goal is to steal, kill, and destroy. Most of the things we worry about and cause us to be fearful or anxious are rooted in lies we learned very early on.

I have a chart that I give to my clients that helps them to identify lies and the entities that are probably involved with those lies. I'm not sure where I got the chart, so I cannot include it in this book. However, it's not as important to know the actual name of an entity as it is to know them by their function. For example: shame. Some of the lies that shame might tell us are, "I'm so stupid,

I shouldn't have done that." "I've gained weight and everyone will think I'm lazy." "I should be a better ___, I'm worthless."

It can be difficult to discover what the exact lie is that you are believing, and that is where an inner healing session could be of benefit. If you have a friend discerning, bold, and courageous enough, they might give you insight as well. However, there is one technique that anyone can do that I have found to be successful.

Ask God to show you or tell you what that lie is. He might give you a picture, or a dream. He might whisper it softly to you. He always speaks with kindness, gentleness, and great love. He wants to rid us of those lies so we can experience the freedom that Jesus died to give us.

Once we discover what the lie is, it's a simple process to break it off: repent, rebuke, kick the enemy out, and declare the truth. So, let's take something obvious as an example, and I'll show you how to break off those lies. Let's say that I believed the lie that "I'm stupid." The base emotion for that lie would be shame, and so that's how we'll identify the enemy involved. I would pray something like this:

Father, forgive me for believing the lie that I'm stupid. I repent of believing that lie, and I revoke all agreement with the spirit of shame. I gather up this spirit of shame, and any others with it, and I cast them on the cross of Jesus. I place the blood of Jesus between all of them and me, and declare that I have the mind of Christ. You created me, and I am intelligent, I am able to learn, and I make good decisions. Father, help me to believe this truth.

Repeat as often as needed.

Sometimes, one round of such a prayer is enough, and the lie doesn't bother us again. We are sure we kicked out that spirit of shame through the authority we have in Christ! With habitual thought patterns, however, we often need to continue to break off the lies and declare the truth over a longer time period. If the lie rears its ugly head again, just repeat the prayer and declaration, and continue to do so until the lie no longer troubles you. Declaring the truth out loud on a frequent basis is another good way to shift those thought patterns.

Here is a vital key to finding victory over negative thoughts–Do NOT allow guilt and condemnation to seep in just because you feel the problem wasn't "fixed" instantly. You've probably believed these lies for a long time and therefore it may take a while to rewire that part of your brain with the truth! The Bible says that God counts up our righteousness and forgets our sins. Let's be more like Him and make note of the times we succeed! Any sort of progress, no matter how small, can be counted as success in my eyes. If that lie used to cross your mind 1000 times a day, you are winning if it only crosses your mind 500 times in a day! If you keep your focus on that win, soon it will be 100 times a day, then 50, then 10, then 5 and then, suddenly, you will find that you rarely, if ever, hear it!

And this, my friend, is freedom indeed!

You might be asking by now, why all the repetition? Through repetition, we are rewiring our brains. Dr. Caroline Leaf has written several fascinating books on the subject of Brain Science. If you want further information, I recommend her books and seminars. If she is scheduled to speak in your area, I encourage you to attend.

Here's a brief summary of her foundational teachings, in my words. Just like a car follows ruts in a road, our brain structures are predisposed to think the things that we have taught it to think. However, those ruts don't have to be permanent, and they can be changed. It might not be easy at first, but it CAN be done! I can attest to this truth as I have seen the fruits of this discipline in my life.

As we speak the truth out loud, we access more areas of our brain than if we were to speak the truth internally. Speaking the truth helps to rewire the new thought structures in our brain, and it then helps to reinforce those new thought structures. Dr. Leaf states that it takes 28 days for a new pathway to form. Just four weeks! That timeframe might depend on how deeply entrenched a particular thought pattern is in your life, however, you should notice a significant difference within 28 days if you are diligent to bind lies and replace them with the truth.

Action Points:
1. Look for areas of your life that seem hopeless.
2. Ask God and/or friends and family what lies you might be believing.
3. Follow the prayer above.
4. Declare the truth.

Bind up the Lies

The thought that is troubling me:

_____

Is there a lie that friends or family say that I believe?

_____
_____
_____
_____

Search the Scriptures to discover what God has to say about this:

_____
_____
_____
_____
_____
_____
_____

What is the truth God saying to ME?

_____
_____
_____
_____
_____
_____

Bind up the Lies

I bind up the lie that:

_____
_____
_____
_____
_____

I repent of believing this lie, and I revoke all agreement with this lie and the spirit(s) of:

_____
_____
_____
_____
_____

I cast this lie to the cross along with any and all entities that are involved in any way. I will not partner with you, and I revoke any and all agreements that I've made with it. I gather all of that up, and I cast it to the cross of Jesus. I place the blood of Jesus between all of that and me, and I accept and choose to believe the truth that:

_____
_____
_____
_____
_____
_____
_____
_____
_____
_____

Read through the prayer of renouncement as often as the lie troubles you. This is very important, especially if the lie is one that plagues you on a consistent basis. Personalize a few Scriptures you found that speak the truth about this lie. Review them as long as it is needed for God's truth to sink in.

Remember, repetition is key to rewire our brains and gain new, healthy habits.

8

FORGIVE QUICKLY AND OFTEN

QUICKLY FORGIVE ANY new offenses that occur against you and continue to forgive those things that try to come back up from your past. Unforgiveness is a serious issue, and one that will hold you in serious bondage. Peter asked Jesus how often he should forgive his brother. Jesus told this parable in answer to the question:

> Then Peter came and said to Him, "Lord, how often shall my brother sin against me and I forgive him? Up to seven times?" Jesus said to him, "I do not say to you, up to seven times, but up to seventy times seven. For this reason the kingdom of heaven may be compared to a king who wished to settle accounts with his slaves. When he had begun to settle them, one who owed him ten thousand talents was brought to him. But since he did not have the means to repay, his lord commanded him to be sold, along with his wife and children and all that he had, and repayment

to be made. So the slave fell to the ground and prostrated himself before him, saying, 'Have patience with me and I will repay you everything.' And the lord of that slave felt compassion and released him and forgave him the debt. But that slave went out and found one of his fellow slaves who owed him a hundred denarii; and he seized him and began to choke him, saying, 'Pay back what you owe.' So his fellow slave fell to the ground and began to plead with him, saying, 'Have patience with me and I will repay you.' But he was unwilling and went and threw him in prison until he should pay back what was owed. So when his fellow slaves saw what had happened, they were deeply grieved and came and reported to their lord all that had happened. Then summoning him, his lord said to him, 'You wicked slave, I forgave you all that debt because you pleaded with me. 'Should you not also have had mercy on your fellow slave, in the same way that I had mercy on you?' And his lord, moved with anger, handed him over to the torturers until he should repay all that was owed him. My heavenly Father will also do the same to you, if each of you does not forgive his brother from your heart." Matthew 18:21-35, NASB

Note–the slave who refused to forgive was handed over to the torturers. Bondage is the natural consequence of not forgiving. Even modern medical practitioners have discovered the truth behind what Jesus alluded to 2000 years ago. Unforgiveness places your body in a state of stress and pressure, and this state can result in diseases of all kinds. Not good!

I grew up with the idea that forgiveness was all or nothing, you either forgave, or you didn't. However, I've since learned that forgiveness is often a process rather than a one-time event, especially for those deep hurts in our lives. Whenever those memories and feelings resurface, we must choose to forgive again. It may be that we are simply reminding ourselves that we chose to forgive, but either way, we might find that we need to forgive more than just once.

Even as you pronounce forgiveness, it's vital to ask God to heal the hurt caused by the offense done against you. Allowing God to bring healing to my heart after I forgave a person was a piece of the puzzle that I missed for quite a while. The principle that nature abhors a vacuum holds true in both the spiritual and natural realms. If there is an empty space, something will try to fill that space. It's not enough to just clean out the bad; we need to flood those areas with the good so we can remain well and live in a place of healing and freedom.

Forgiveness is primarily a transaction between you and God, and not necessarily between you and the person. In general, it is a good idea to go to the person and express your forgiveness, however, depending on the circumstances, that might not be wise or safe. Just because you forgive someone, it does not necessarily mean that trust must be restored, and that relationship is healed. If a person has repeatedly shown themselves to be untrustworthy, you can forgive them while maintaining healthy boundaries. Forgiveness doesn't mean that everything is okay between you and those who hurt you. It means that you are set free from holding the other person responsible, you are giving that responsibility to Christ and being free of the torment of unforgiveness!

Action Points:
1. Think about any people that have hurt you in the past, or present.
2. Declare that you are choosing to forgive them.
3. Keep reminding yourself that you have chosen to forgive them when they come to mind.
4. Rejoice that forgiveness is your get out of jail free card!

Forgiveness Worksheet: Setting Yourself Free!

Please note: this is not to be an exercise in stirring up the bitterness. Do not dwell on the wrongs that were done to you. Summarize them and then move on to forgiveness. I provide the following as a template, but I'd recommend that you make a copy of this template and fill it in for each person that comes to mind, or jot down your answers on a separate piece of paper.

Who hurt me? (Name is optional) _____

BRIEFLY, what did they do?

_____
_____

My prayer: Father or Jesus, I forgive _____ for _____
_____
_____

I release them and their wounds from my life, and I set myself free from the hold that bitterness and unforgiveness has had in my life because of this. I speak a blessing over their life.

Repeat the steps for whoever comes readily to mind. Extra worksheets follow.

Now, tear up these papers, and/or burn them (if you can safely do so) as a prophetic act. As you do so, you are releasing your forgiveness toward those who hurt you and you are releasing yourself from the wounds of the past. Repeat as needed.

Who hurt me? (Name is optional) _____

BRIEFLY, what did they do?

_____
_____

My prayer: Father or Jesus, I forgive _____ for _____
_____
_____

I release them and their wounds from my life, and I set myself free from the hold that bitterness and unforgiveness has had in my life because of this. I speak a blessing over their life.

Repeat the steps for whoever comes readily to mind. Extra worksheets follow.

Now, tear up these papers, and/or burn them (if you can safely do so) as a prophetic act. As you do so, you are releasing your forgiveness toward those who hurt you and you are releasing yourself from the wounds of the past. Repeat as needed.

Who hurt me? (Name is optional) _____

BRIEFLY, what did they do?

_____
_____

My prayer: Father or Jesus, I forgive _____ for _____
_____
_____

I release them and their wounds from my life, and I set myself free from the hold that bitterness and unforgiveness has had in my life because of this. I speak a blessing over their life.

Repeat the steps for whoever comes readily to mind. Extra worksheets follow.

Now, tear up these papers, and/or burn them (if you can safely do so) as a prophetic act. As you do so, you are releasing your forgiveness toward those who hurt you and you are releasing yourself from the wounds of the past. Repeat as needed.

Who hurt me? (Name is optional) _____

BRIEFLY, what did they do?

_____
_____

My prayer: Father or Jesus, I forgive _____ for _____
_____
_____

I release them and their wounds from my life, and I set myself free from the hold that bitterness and unforgiveness has had in my life because of this. I speak a blessing over their life.

Repeat the steps for whoever comes readily to mind. Extra worksheets follow.

Now, tear up these papers, and/or burn them (if you can safely do so) as a prophetic act. As you do so, you are releasing your forgiveness toward those who hurt you and you are releasing yourself from the wounds of the past. Repeat as needed.

Who hurt me? (Name is optional) _____

BRIEFLY, what did they do?

_____
_____

My prayer: Father or Jesus, I forgive _____ for _____
_____
_____

I release them and their wounds from my life, and I set myself free from the hold that bitterness and unforgiveness has had in my life because of this. I speak a blessing over their life.

Repeat the steps for whoever comes readily to mind. Extra worksheets follow.

Now, tear up these papers, and/or burn them (if you can safely do so) as a prophetic act. As you do so, you are releasing your forgiveness toward those who hurt you and you are releasing yourself from the wounds of the past. Repeat as needed.

9

A COMMUNITY OF BELIEVERS

THE FOLLOWING CHAPTER might be difficult for some of my readers but stay with me. We all need other people in our lives. The extroverted among us need people more often than those of us who are introverted, but the necessity of community is universal. While it is not always easy, it is important to find a group with whom you can connect in a meaningful way. We all need people in our lives that know us well and are who are able and willing to speak into our lives. We were not created to do life alone. God, Himself, was not content with just being the Trinity; He created humans for friendship's sake.

Many who are looking for a group of believers to do life with might consider Church the typical place to find such a group. I write this with some trepidation because I know that for many of us, the church has been the place where we experienced our greatest woundings. The body of Christ can be vicious to its own. However, in this chapter, I'm referring to a broader concept of the church, I am not just referring to the building you might go to on a Sunday morning.

How do we go about finding people to be in relationship with, people who are like-minded believers? Being like-minded doesn't mean they all think exactly like you. I find that to be very dull. I enjoy hearing and learning about different perspectives. However, it is important to at least have a sense you share the same solid foundation on the basics of what you believe and the direction you want to head. If I wish to become more like Christ, then I need to align myself with others on the same path.

You might find others with whom you can align yourself with in a home church, a small Bible study, a local house of prayer, or something of that nature. Ask God to show you where to go and with whom to connect. A term I have heard bantered about as of late is 'Micro-church.' If you can't find one, maybe you can start one! Gather with a friend or two and watch a webcast of a service, and then talk about it over lunch. It doesn't have to be formal, and you don't need to do the same thing every time you meet.

It's important to realize that people are not perfect, Christian or not. If we are expecting them to be, then we are a part of the problem. Should Christians be better at loving others? Absolutely! Jesus is our example and the one we should emulate. But none of us get it right all of the time. So, forgive and extend grace when needed. Try to do your best to love others, believers or not, and to love them well. I'm referring here to extending grace and patience for honest mistakes; I am not referring to enabling toxic patterns of behavior in others.

Not all groups are safe places, and we should carefully choose the one we wish to attend. Some leaders are controlling and manipulative and should be avoided. Some tolerate toxic behavior from group members. If you run across one of those, try somewhere else. Thankfully, such toxic groups are not the norm. Mistakes are bound to happen in any group but pay attention to how those mistakes are dealt with by leadership. A healthy community is learning and growing, even within its imperfections.

It might take time to find the right group, and it might take time to develop a relationship with the people in that group. Don't give up too quickly. If the group appears to be healthy, and the group is made up of people who are encouraging one another to grow, and you have some things in common, then give it time to become your place of connection. By giving it some time, I don't just mean passively putting in your time, but I mean time spent interacting with those in the group!

As a person who has been very introverted (I'm slowly growing into more of an ambivert), I know all too well the temptation just to go and sit in a corner and call that good enough. Unfortunately, I also know from experience that this does not work well at all!

Think about the size of the group you are considering joining. For most introverts, smaller is better. If you tend to feel lost in a crowd, a mega church might not be your best option. Even extroverts need a few core people who know them well, even if others with whom they have a surface relationship surround them.

We all need individuals in our lives who support us in our healing journey, and who are there to do life with. We need people who encourage our relationship with God, and for whom we can do the same. If you find several such people, that's even better! They may take some searching to find, but these gems will be worth the effort to find!

Action Points:

1. Pray about joining a community or gathering of believers.
2. Is there someone in your life who you think you could encourage in their faith and be encouraged by?
3. See if there is a house of prayer or something similar near you and attend if possible.
4. If at first you don't succeed, try again. It can just take a while to find people of like mind, don't become discouraged if you don't have a good experience everywhere you go!

I know that for many Christians, their deepest hurts were inflicted through the actions of people within the church. I think that this is one of the saddest things ever, and I'm confident that it breaks Jesus' heart. The people who should be the most like Him, so often aren't. I've received a few stabs in the back from 'church people,' and I know how it goes. I've not found any official statistics to back up my findings, but I'm willing to wager a guess, based on my highly scientific observations on Facebook. There are more who have been hurt by fellow believers, than those who have not hurt at some point by fellow believers in their Christian walk. This isn't a game to discover who has been more severely wounded; it's about finding freedom.

You may be saying, "But Alice! You don't understand what happened to me!" And that's true; I don't. But, here's the thing. I don't need to know all the details for you to be set free. Jesus was there. He knows. He saw. Moreover, He knows what that offense did to you and how deeply it hurt your heart. He can help you through this.

Perhaps you've gone through the forgiveness exercises in the previous chapter. Go back and use the template provided to work through any unforgiveness that might still linger toward situations around church or church people. If you have not yet worked through that chapter, I encourage you to do so.

Those situations where forgiveness needs to be released might not have happened at church. You might have worked with people who professed to be Christians but did not act very Christ-like on the job. Regardless of how the wounds were inflicted upon you, I would like to make an apology to you on behalf of Christians, and the church in general. I am willing to repent on behalf of those who hurt you. Would you be willing to accept my apology? Here goes:

I apologize to you, today, as a Christian, a church goer, one who has held leadership positions in the church, and one who has not always behaved in a manner pleasing to my Jesus. I apologize on behalf of all who have hurt you in the name of the church or the name of Christianity. I'm so sorry that you were hurt. I'm so sorry that you felt unloved, unworthy, or anything else negative. Please accept my apology and be free from the wounds inflicted on you by others like me. I speak a blessing over you from my position stated above. You are free to receive the love and the acceptance that Jesus so freely gives to us all. He loves you and died just for you so that you can be free.

Forgiveness Worksheet–Groups, Churches, etc.

Setting Yourself Free!

This is not to be an exercise in stirring up the bitterness. Do not dwell on the wrongs that were done to you. Summarize and move on to forgiveness. I recommend that you make a physical copy of this sheet, or jot down your answers to the questions below on a separate piece of paper.

Who hurt me? (Group, church, etc) _____

BRIEFLY, what did they do?

_____
_____

My prayer: Father or Jesus, I forgive _____ for _____
_____
_____

I release them and their wounds from my life, and I set myself free from the hold that bitterness and unforgiveness has had in my life because of this. I speak a blessing over their life.

Repeat for whatever group comes readily to mind.

Now, tear up these papers, and/or burn them (if you can safely do so) as a prophetic act. As you do so, you are releasing your forgiveness toward those who hurt you and you are releasing yourself from the wounds of the past. Repeat as needed.

Who hurt me? (Group, church, etc) _____

BRIEFLY, what did they do?

_____
_____

My prayer: Father or Jesus, I forgive _____ for _____
_____
_____

I release them and their wounds from my life, and I set myself free from the hold that bitterness and unforgiveness has had in my life because of this. I speak a blessing over their life.

Repeat for whatever group comes readily to mind.

Now, tear up these papers, and/or burn them (if you can safely do so) as a prophetic act. As you do so, you are releasing your forgiveness toward those who hurt you and you are releasing yourself from the wounds of the past. Repeat as needed.

A Community of Believers

Who hurt me? (Group, church, etc) _____

BRIEFLY, what did they do?

_____
_____

My prayer: Father or Jesus, I forgive _____ for _____
_____
_____

I release them and their wounds from my life, and I set myself free from the hold that bitterness and unforgiveness has had in my life because of this. I speak a blessing over their life.

Repeat for whatever group comes readily to mind.

Now, tear up these papers, and/or burn them (if you can safely do so) as a prophetic act. As you do so, you are releasing your forgiveness toward those who hurt you and you are releasing yourself from the wounds of the past. Repeat as needed.

Who hurt me? (Group, church, etc) _____

BRIEFLY, what did they do?

_____
_____

My prayer: Father or Jesus, I forgive _____ for _____
_____
_____

I release them and their wounds from my life, and I set myself free from the hold that bitterness and unforgiveness has had in my life because of this. I speak a blessing over their life.

Repeat for whatever group comes readily to mind.

Now, tear up these papers, and/or burn them (if you can safely do so) as a prophetic act. As you do so, you are releasing your forgiveness toward those who hurt you and you are releasing yourself from the wounds of the past. Repeat as needed.

10

EXERCISE YOUR SPIRITUAL GIFTINGS

THERE ARE SEVERAL online tests that can help you to identify your spiritual giftings. My personal opinion is that while these tests are good as far as they go, any and all giftings can be utilized by the Spirit. Ephesians 2:10 says, "For we are His workmanship, created in Christ Jesus for good works, which God prepared beforehand so that we would walk in them." (NASB)

In this chapter, I'm going to cast my net a bit broader than what is typically covered in online spiritual gifts tests. I'll use myself as an example. The painting above is one I created during worship. I have found that I connect the best to God and feel his pleasure the most when I am engaged in creative pursuits.

The only time that I don't connect with God and feel His pleasure as I use my giftings is when I have bought into a lie, or when I have some other sin issue that is hindering my relationship with God. So that's my cue to seek

His face, and discover what it is the source of the disconnect and get rid of it. I believe that this principle is true for anyone, whatever their particular gifting might be. For example, it might usually be easy for us to serve others, to teach, to solve problems, or to do whatever it is typically a strong skill set for us. However, there might be times when these things don't come as quickly as they once did. It's helpful when those times arise to make sure that there is nothing within us that hinders us from serving God and others with our giftings.

Our giftings keep us connected to the greater body of Christ, as we discussed in the last chapter. Operating in our giftings helps us to take the focus off of ourselves and place it on others around us, no matter where we find ourselves utilizing our gifts. Going back to my example, I believe that God releases more of what He wants to release in a gathering of believers through the creation of art in that meeting. When I post my work online, or when I paint in the midst of a gathering of God's people, I allow others to benefit from my encounter with God. To follow my creative adventures, you can follow me at alicearlene.com

Going back to my discussion of spiritual gift tests, I have never seen creative pursuits listed as a possible gift mix on any such test. Don't limit your understanding of what spiritual giftings are by what might or might not be listed on generic tests. I would encourage you to ask the Lord what your spiritual giftings are during a journaling session or quiet time. Then go one step further. Just don't ask what your giftings might be, but ask God how He would like you to use them.

Note that I'm using the plural "giftings" here. I have yet to meet someone who only had one gift. If one gift is all you can think of right now, that's fine. Rock that gifting as best you can. Just don't be surprised when you discover other gifts along the way. There are some giftings that surface only when they are needed in certain situations. Some gifts will become more prominent as you walk in more of the freedom God has given you.

Action Points:
1. What is your spiritual gift?
2. What comes easily or naturally to you?
3. How can you invite God into this task? How can you use this task to join with Him as He blesses others?

Spiritual Giftings Worksheet

What are any of my known spiritual gifts?

_____
_____
_____
_____
_____

What comes easily or naturally for me?

_____
_____
_____
_____
_____

Gift 1: _____

How can this gift be used to demonstrate the love of the Father, or to build up others, within the church, or outside the church? Dream big here! In a perfect world where you had all the time and money and resources you ever needed at your disposal, how could you use that gift?

_____
_____
_____
_____
_____
_____
_____
_____

What are some things that you can do right now, given your time, abilities, money, or other constraints:

_____
_____
_____
_____
_____

Choose one of the things you just listed in the last question. Circle or highlight it. Ask yourself, "When am I going to act on this? How am I going to do it?" Mark this on your calendar.

_____
_____
_____
_____
_____

Do you need to purchase supplies? Make a list of things to gather or purchase:

_____
_____
_____
_____
_____
_____
_____
_____
_____
_____
_____

Gift 2: _____

How can this gift be used to demonstrate the love of the Father, or to build up others, within the church, or outside the church? Dream big here! In a perfect world where you had all the time and money and resources you ever needed at your disposal, how could you use that gift?

_____
_____
_____
_____
_____

What are some things that you can do right now, given your time, abilities, money, or other constraints:

_____
_____
_____
_____
_____

Choose one of the things you just listed in the last question. Circle or highlight it. Ask yourself, "When am I going to act on this? How am I going to do it?" Mark this on your calendar.

_____
_____
_____
_____
_____
_____

Do you need to purchase supplies? Make a list of things to gather or purchase:

_____
_____
_____
_____
_____
_____
_____
_____
_____
_____

Gift 3: _____

How can this gift be used to demonstrate the love of the Father, or to build up others, within the church, or outside the church? Dream big here! In a perfect world where you had all the time and money and resources you ever needed at your disposal, how could you use that gift?

_____
_____
_____
_____
_____

What are some things that you can do right now, given your time, abilities, money, or other constraints:

_____
_____
_____
_____
_____

Choose one of the things you just listed in the last question. Circle or highlight it. Ask yourself, "When am I going to act on this? How am I going to do it?" Mark this on your calendar.

_____
_____
_____
_____
_____

Do you need to purchase supplies? Make a list of things to gather or purchase:

_____
_____
_____
_____
_____
_____
_____

11

PRACTICE THANKFULNESS

I'LL BE DISCUSSING thankfulness in this, the last but certainly not the least, chapter of the "Guide to Freedom." Thankfulness might be defined as the act of consciously looking for things to be grateful for, and looking for all the good you can find.

Thankfulness is a powerful tool for a Christian. The enemy knows this and attempts to defeat you by making negative things around you seem larger than they are. He knows that if he can keep you focused on negativity, you will miss all of the good that is around you. Thankfulness trains you to learn to look for and to find the positive things that are happening in your life.

Obviously, there are bad things that happen from time to time. I am not recommending or suggesting that you should be in denial when bad things happen. There are some who teach that if you make any acknowledgement of negative things, you give those negative things access to your life. I am not one who holds to that specific view. Our words do have power, and should be used with care. However, some take this principle to an extreme, creating a superstitious fear of the power of negative words.

For example, if I have a large amount of money stolen from me, I can choose to focus on the theft of the money, or I can choose to be thankful that I still have a roof over my head and food to eat. I'm not in denial that the lost money would have been helpful to have, but my focus is on moving forward despite the loss.

When developing a thankfulness mindset, it's useful to review your day every evening and make note of the positive things that happened during that day. Large and small, make note of every single positive thing you can remember. Some people jot down the most significant item of each day on a slip of paper, and then place the paper into a jar or box. They then can periodically review them.

Look for ways that you can be of help to others around you as you go about your day. A friend was in a tough work situation, and I suggested that she look for some way that God could use her in her workplace every day. Sometimes we get so overwhelmed by the big issues that we don't see the good things that we can do. While it is important to see the big picture, we need balance! We mustn't overlook the small everyday good things. By looking for ways in which we can be a blessing to others, we turn our focus outward, and we are then able to be thankful that we have the ability to do whatever it is that we can do.

Teaching ourselves to look for the good is an excellent coping strategy. Even during very dark times, the darkness will not overwhelm us because we can still see the light.

Action Points:
1. Name one thing that you have to be thankful for.
2. Make a thankfulness jar or box.
3. Put things you have to be thankful for in the box.
4. Review the items in the box any time you are having a hard time finding something to be thankful for, or set a regular schedule to review those items, perhaps on a weekly, monthly, or yearly basis.

5. This would be a great activity in which to utilize a bullet journal. Make a list sheet or find a calendar that has enough room for you to list at least three items every day. Every night, write as many things as you can that you are thankful for. Big or small, just write them down. As you go throughout your day, look for things that you can write down that night.
6. Create a thankfulness box by using any box that you like. An empty cereal box, or tissue box, or whatever you have handy will work just fine. You can decorate it as you like. If you have kids, this is a great activity to do with them. Once the box is decorated, each of you can place something in the box. Age appropriate expressions of thankfulness might include drawings that depict what they are thankful for, or a note they write themselves. You could also write a note dictated by your preschoolers and have them place their special thankfulness note in the box by themselves. If you start with a small box, however, be prepared to upsize that box as your thankfulness grows!
7. There's something about looking for something that sets us up for finding what we are looking for. If we are looking for things to be thankful for, then we will begin to see them everywhere. Some speak about manifesting your intention, but I'm not so sure that's actually what happens. I might describe this process as training your reticular activating system (a part of your brain) to spot what it is that you want. This works both ways! If you are looking for the bad, than you will surely find it, but if you look for the good, why, it's everywhere! I'm not saying that everything will be all peaches and cream and roses. No, difficulties will still arise. However, I firmly believe that practicing thankfulness will help you thrive despite circumstances. You won't just squeak by through life.

TODAY, I AM THANKFUL FOR:

TODAY, I AM THANKFUL FOR:

TODAY, I AM THANKFUL FOR:

TODAY, I AM THANKFUL FOR:

TODAY, I AM THANKFUL FOR:

TODAY, I AM THANKFUL FOR:

12

A BRIEF DISCUSSION OF SPLANKNA AND SOZO

EVERYONE EXPERIENCES TROUBLES, hard times, disappointments, failures, and setbacks. What you do with those experiences ultimately determines how emotionally and spiritually healthy you will be in the future. When we experience trauma of any type, we tend to store those negative emotions in our physical being. We believe lies about ourselves and lies about those around us. These emotions and lies tend to 'trigger' us and we react in ways that are not logical or desirable. Sometimes these issues hinder us from moving forward as we subconsciously sabotage our progress towards the things we most desire.

Most of the time, we are able to work through these types of issues on our own. However, there are times where we feel stuck and we need a little help to break through into our next level of freedom and peace. Working with others, we are able to quickly release emotional and spiritual baggage that might be hindering our progress.

I work as a facilitator and my work is grounded in Christian principles. I guide my clients as they release painful emotions, lies, and heartaches that trigger unwanted symptoms. I help them to rediscover who God is and what He has to say to and about them. Trained in both Splankna and Sozo techniques for inner and energy healing, I believe the Holy Spirit is our healer and He will guide my clients on a journey towards complete emotional and spiritual healing.

Inner Healing

The process of healing the emotional and spiritual wounds that we all encounter during life is called many things. Inner Healing is a broad term often used to describe this process. It encompasses an area of our lives that is usually not addressed by more traditional methods of healing. We are learning more and more about the inner-connectedness of our beings: mind, body, emotions; spirit and soul. It is becoming clearer in many streams of inner healing work that many physical complaints can find their roots in emotional and spiritual issues. While inner healing cannot guarantee relief from physical ailments, many people find a marked improvement in their physical health as they experience healing of their emotional and spiritual wounds.

Although there are many anecdotal reports of great benefit, and all of these modalities appear to show great promise of benefit to people emotionally, spiritually, and even physically; they have yet to be fully researched by Western medical, academic, and psychological communities. Therefore, they are considered experimental, and the extent of their benefits (which appear to be many) and their risks (which appear to be minimal) are not entirely known.

However, unlike the traditional Western medicine's view, I believe modalities and treatment protocols should be highly individualized. Therefore, no two sessions that I facilitate are the same even with the same client with the same issue. Are there similarities of issues? Yes, of course. We all share in the same human condition. However, many variables come into play in a person's life. I think that this is the aspect of healing that fascinates me the most! These variables present a clear and distinct demonstration that God created each of us uniquely. He knows each of us very well, much better than we know ourselves.

What does a session look like?

I begin each session with prayer with my client, asking God to guide the session, as only He truly knows what needs to be addressed and how that will bring about the greatest healing. We then follow His lead throughout the session, bringing increased healing and wholeness to the areas He points out by utilizing the tools I've learned. I remain ever mindful of His leading. Throughout each session, I lead my client in prayers in Jesus' Name, as He is our access point to the Father and the Holy Spirit. While it is not necessary for my clients to believe in God, prayer is the foundation of my work, so a willingness to receive prayer in this manner is necessary. A session is a collaboration between my client, God, and I. They are encouraged to ask questions throughout the session if there is anything that is unclear.

Splankna

Splankna Therapy is the first Christian protocol for energy psychology. Energy psychology utilizes the same system in the body that acupuncture and chiropractic utilizes. It does so to alleviate emotional trauma that is physically stored within the body. The Splankna Protocol incorporates elements from three different energy psychology protocols: Thought Field Therapy, EMDR (Eye Movement Desensitization and Reprocessing), and Neuro-Emotional Technique. Splankna also incorporates prayer as an integral part of every session.

I am a Master's Level Certified Splankna Practitioner. I appreciate this technique, as it seems to address issues at the subconscious and energetic levels. Using applied kinesiology to assist in identifying the problem, the protocol then assists my client to release any negative emotions that are stored within their physical being that might be triggering a current symptom. Once emotional "fuel" is released, there is nothing left to trigger the symptom, and they are then free to make better behavioral choices.

To learn more about Splankna and how it works, please visit the Splankna Therapy Institute page splankna.com. There is an audio file on their website that includes a basic presentation of the Splankna protocol of Christian energy healing. The presentation also addresses theological questions and justifications.

Sozo

Sozo is a Greek word translated into English as "saved, healed, and delivered." Sozo is a unique inner healing and deliverance ministry aimed at finding the root of those things that hinder personal connections with the Father, Son, and Holy Spirit. Once that connection is restored, you can walk in the destiny to which you have been called. Sozo is not a counseling session per say; it is a time of interacting with Father, Son, and Holy Spirit as you pursue wholeness and release of your destiny. The incredible people at Bethel Church in Redding, California developed Sozo inner healing techniques.

I am trained at the Advanced Sozo level. While I am not a member of the Sozo Network, I utilize many of their techniques. I have found them to be useful when establishing a strong connection between you and God. Sozo encourages us to have an encounter with each member of the Godhead. By doing so, we reinforce a healthy sense of identity as we hear what God thinks about us from God Himself.For more information about this technique, please visit bethelsozo.com.

For those of you who are already working with a practitioner, you might or might not be familiar with some of these methods I have discussed. These are by no means the only modalities of inner healing out there, and I encourage you to continue your work with your practitioner.

If you are not familiar with inner healing work, all this may be revolutionary information for you. I would encourage you to investigate options near you and seek out a practitioner. If you are unable to find one, feel free to contact me to arrange for either an in-person session, or a Skype session. In-person sessions are preferable. However, Skype is an option for those of you who do not live near Lubbock, TX and are unable to travel here for an intensive session. Please note that Skype sessions will not involve muscle testing, but I will be listening to God and discerning what tools to use, based on your presenting issues.

ABOUT THE AUTHOR

Alice Briggs is an inner healing practitioner, artist, author, and teacher. She resides in Texas with her family. Through difficulties in her own life, she discovered the power that lies in these simple, yet profound, changes to increase her joy, hope, and peace. She shares them with you here in the hopes that you will experience victory and success in all areas of your life.

www.emotionalandspiritualhealing.com

Books are available whereever books are sold.

ACCESSING YOUR SPIRITUAL INHERITANCE

Alice Briggs, Del Hungerford & Seneca Schurbon

It's Your Turn to Go Through the Door

Alice didn't fall down a rabbit hole, she walked through a mystical doorway in a vision to recover blessings her ancestors had not claimed.

When Alice came back and shared her experience, Seneca wasted no time going through her own door.

Del's approach differed — she wound up floating along in her bloodstream!

Using the map we give in our stories, others went through their own doors leading to better relationships with God and increases in finances, favor, and giftings.

Although this book touches on generational curses and how to remove them, we focus on claiming the blessings your family line has lost.

If you're open to having a vision or seeing in the spirit, we'll walk you through the step-by-step process of learning to see, so you, too, can restore your lost generational blessings.

Your hidden inheritance awaits!

EMOTIONAL AND SPIRITUAL HEALING SERIES

Alice Briggs

Fourteen books on how to heal from the most common negative emotions from the past that effect your present and future happiness and success.

Overcoming Perfection
Overcoming Rejection
Overcoming Shame
Overcoming Anxiety
Overcoming Insecurity
Overcoming Anger
Overcoming Hopelessness
Overcoming Control
Overcoming Triggers
Overcoming Guilt
Overcoming Confusion
Overcoming Grief
Overcoming Jealousy
Overcoming Pride

www.ingramcontent.com/pod-product-compliance
Lightning Source LLC
Chambersburg PA
CBHW072058290426
44110CB00014B/1740